S0-BSA-722

The Faith & Vision of

BENJAMIN

FRANKLIN

*How the Skeptical Printer of Philadelphia
Returned to His Puritan Roots &
The Puritan Vision
For a Christian America*

Eddie L. Hyatt

Hyatt Press * 2015
Renewing Minds – Changing Hearts

THE FAITH OF BENJAMIN FRANKLIN
*How the Skeptical Printer of Philadelphia Returned to His
Puritan Roots & the Puritan Vision for a Christian America*
By Eddie L. Hyatt

© 2015 by Hyatt International Ministries, Incorporated.
ALL RIGHTS RESERVED.

Published by Hyatt Press
A Subsidiary of Hyatt Int'l Ministries, Incorporated.

Mailing Address (2015)
Hyatt Int'l Ministries
P. O. Box 3877
Grapevine (Dallas-Fort Worth Metroplex), TX 76099

Internet Addresses
Email: *dreddiehyatt@gmail.com*
Web Sites: *www.eddiehyatt.com*

Unless otherwise indicated, all Scripture quotations are
taken from the New Kings James Version of the Bible.
© 1979, 1980, 1982 by Thomas Nelson, Inc. Publishers.

ISBN 978-1-888435-54-2

Printed in the United States of America

Endorsements

As always, Eddie Hyatt, brings us a well-researched history book that reads as pleasurably as a novel. Benjamin Franklin has been so used and abused by revisionists who want us to doubt the spiritual beginnings of the United States of America. I have so enjoyed this account of Franklin's faith which is something of a restoration of this founding father's reputation as a believer. George Whitefield, is my friend by means of studying his part in The Great Awakening out of which this country was birthed. How wonderful to know, *via* Hyatt's book, that he was also a longtime friend of Benjamin Franklin.

Billye Brim
Billye Brim Ministries

Secularists are always pooh-poohing we Christians' contention that the major Founding Fathers were all religious believers. My friend Eddie Hyatt with books like this one adds scholarly heft to our contention. And he proves that even the supposedly Deist Benjamin Franklin knew not only that God had a hand in our nation's affairs, but believed He SHOULD. So take that, secularists! Read this book, study the quotes and footnotes, and find out once and for all what a fervent believer Ben was.

Paul Strand
CBN News
Senior Washington Correspondent

Eddie Hyatt shines a new light on one of America's most significant founders, Benjamin Franklin, by shedding "politically-correct" presuppositions and taking a fresh look at the history behind the man. By chronicling Franklin's spiritual journey, Hyatt uncovers the American patriarch's progression from Puritanism, through Deism, to the Great Awakening, and finally his return to his Christian roots. Every believer interested in "His-Story" should read The Faith of Benjamin Franklin and discover another reason why America is "one nation under God"!

Anne Gimenez
Rock Ministerial Fellowship

I have known Drs. Eddie & Susan Hyatt intimately for more than thirty years as people of integrity in their lives, ministry, and scholarship. I always look forward to their next book and could hardly wait to download this new one on Franklin when they sent me the manuscript. I was not disappointed. It is expertly written and easy to read. I highly recommend this book to everyone who is interested in knowing America's true Christian origins.

Valarie Owen
Ministry of Faith and
Calvary Cathedral International Bible College

About the Author

Dr. Eddie L. Hyatt is a seasoned minister of the Gospel, having served as a pastor, teacher, missionary, and professor of theology in the U.S. and Canada and having ministered in India, Indonesia, England, Ireland, Sweden, Poland, and Bulgaria. His ministry is characterized by a unique blend of the anointing of the Holy Spirit and academic excellence and over 40 years of ministerial experience.

Eddie has made a life-long commitment to the study of Scripture, church history, and Spiritual renewal. He holds a Doctor of Ministry from Regent University, where he majored in church history and spiritual renewal. He also holds the Master of Divinity and a Master of Arts in Historical-Theology from Oral Roberts University.

Eddie has lectured on revival, church history and various Biblical themes in churches, conferences, and some of the major educational institutions in the world today. These include Oxford University in England, Doulos Bible College in India, Oral Roberts University, Zion Bible College, Christ For the Nations Institute, and others. He has authored several books, including the highly acclaimed *2000 Years of Charismatic Christianity*, which is used as a textbook in colleges and seminaries around the world.

Eddie recently founded "Revive America" for the purpose of demonstrating America's radical Christian origins and calling for a return to the nation's founding principles by means of another great Spiritual awakening.

He resides in Grapevine, TX, where he and his wife, Dr. Susan Hyatt, carry on a ministry of teaching, preaching, writing, video and TV production, and publishing. To learn more of his ministry, visit www.eddiehyatt.com.

Mailing Address
  Eddie L. Hyatt
  P. O. Box 3877
  Grapevine, TX 76088

Online Connections
  ➤ *Email:* DrEddieHyatt@gmail.com
  ➤ *Web Site:* www.EddieHyatt.com
  ➤ *Blog:* www.BiblicalAwakening.com
  ➤ *Face Book:* FaceBook.com/dreddiehyatt
  ➤ *Twitter:* https://twitter.com/EddieHyatt
  ➤ *YouTube:* YouTube.com/user/ReviveAmericaNow

Table of Contents

Preface

In a letter dated July 2, 1756, Benjamin Franklin presented a proposal to George Whitefield, the most famous preacher of the Great Awakening, proposing that they partner to establish a Christian colony "in the Ohio," which was frontier country at the time.

Franklin had become friends with Whitefield 17 years prior to this, when Whitefield visited Philadelphia and preached to massive outdoor crowds. Franklin attended the meetings and took on the task of printing and distributing Whitefield's sermons. Although they were different in many ways, the skeptical American printer and the fiery British evangelist hit it off in what proved to be the beginning of a close, life-long friendship.

In the 1756 letter, Franklin expressed his belief that by establishing such a colony with a "strong body of religious and industrious people," the other colonies would be made more secure and commerce would be increased.

Franklin also presented a missionary reason for such a colony, saying that it "would greatly facilitate the introduction of pure religion among the heathen," referring to the American Indians in the area. They could be evangelized, Franklin suggested, by showing them "a better sample of Christians than they commonly see." He expressed confidence that God would give them success in such a project, "if we undertook it with a sincere regard to his honor."[1]

Although time and circumstances did not allow them the opportunity to launch this project, I will argue in the following pages that Franklin's vision for a Christian society never died, but was fulfilled in the founding of the United States of America, of which he was one of the most important Founding Fathers.

Modern secularists love to present Franklin as a nonreligious Deist who wanted to keep Christianity out of the public domain. Such a view of Franklin, however, is based on selected quotations, without regard for his changing views on God and Christianity as he matured. Such a view also ignores his Puritan heritage and his close friendship with devout believers, particularly his friendship with George Whitefield.

Indeed, the modern secularist who wants to strip the public square of every vestige of Christian influence will find no friend in the real Benjamin Franklin.

I have written this book for a general audience and have relied primarily on Franklin's own words found in his *Autobiography*. I have also utilized a few, selected sources, listed in the endnotes, and chosen because of the authors' integrity, objectivity and scholarship. Two that were particularly valuable in the writing of this book are *George Whitefield, America's Spiritual Founding Father* by Thomas S. Kidd and *Faith & Freedom* by Benjamin Hart.

Chapter I

Born and Reared in a Christian Home

> *As I speak of thanking God, I desire with all humility to acknowledge that I attribute the mentioned happiness of my past life to his divine providence.*
> Benjamin Franklin

Benjamin Franklin was born in Boston, MA, on January 17, 1706, into a hard-working, Protestant family with Puritan values and influences on both sides of the family. He was baptized at the Old South Meeting House, a Puritan Church that is now a famous historical landmark in downtown Boston.

His Puritan Heritage

Puritanism was not a church or denomination, but was, instead, a renewal movement that began in England with those seeking to reform the Church of England, similar to what had happened through Martin Luther in Germany and Ulrich Zwingli in Switzerland. Puritans took the Bible, rather than a pope or bishop, as their ultimate guide and preached a personal faith that could not only be known in the head, but also experienced in the heart.

The movement gained significant momentum in 17th century England. Its intellectual center was at Cambridge University, where Puritan professors and theologians wrote and published books and tracts on religious liberty and the proper roles of the church and civil government.

Because the movement challenged the hierarchical structure of the state church, Puritans came under severe persecution. This was especially true of the separatist Puritans who left the Church of England and began forming "illegal" congregations. Among these people were the Pilgrims who landed at Cape Cod in November of 1620. They came to America to escape persecution from the civil and religious authorities in England.

His Father Fled Religious Persecution

The evidence suggests that Franklin's forebears were separatist Puritans on both sides of the family. He refers to them as "dissenting Protestants," and he tells how his father, Josiah Franklin, fled England in 1685 with his first wife and three small children in order to escape religious persecution. In his *Autobiography*, Franklin says they came under persecution in England because of their attendance at "conventicles," which were religious gatherings that had been outlawed by the government.

A "conventicle" was simply any religious meeting that was not sanctioned by the Church of England. The Conventicle Act of 1670 was passed by Parliament to put pressure on the many religious, separatist groups that were arising in England at the time. These included separatist Puritans, Quakers, Baptists, and others. Franklin says his father brought his young family to America "where they expected to enjoy the exercise of their religion with freedom."[2]

Josiah's first wife died while still young, and he married Abiah Folger. Together they had ten children, with Benjamin being the youngest son. Abiah's father—Benjamin's grandfather—Peter Folger, was among the first Puritan settlers in New England. Folger was a staunch defender of religious liberty, and when the Puritans of Boston persecuted Quakers and Baptists who came into their midst, Folger wrote several works defending the Quakers and Baptists on the basis of religious liberty.

The Puritan Work Ethic

Modern secular historians have sought to denigrate the Puritans by seizing upon certain extremes that occurred at times within their ranks, and using these in an attempt to stereotype the entire movement. On the contrary, for the most part, the Puritans were good, Christian people seeking to follow Christ at a very difficult time in history. In England, many suffered imprisonment for their faith, and some gave their lives rather than deny their faith in Christ.

The Puritans became known, not only for their faith, but also for their frugality and diligent work ethic, and these qualities abounded in the family into which Franklin was born. This work ethic had much to do with the reason and motivation for the Puritan immigration to the New World.

A major difference between the Puritans and earlier settlers and explorers is that the Puritans came, not for gold and adventure, but to develop a godly society and create a new life. Whereas even the earlier Anglican settlement at Jamestown in 1607 consisted only of men and was tainted by the desire for adventure and personal gain, the Puritan immigration, beginning in 1620, consisted of entire families—husbands, wives, children, and in some cases, even their livestock. Out of both purpose and necessity, they focused on building a life for their families in the New World.

During the week, Josiah worked long hours at his trade as a candle-maker and used mealtime as an opportunity for teaching his children though open, family discussions. Franklin recalled that his father would often invite a wise friend or astute neighbor to share a meal and converse on a particular topic of importance and interest, always focused on matters of faith, diligence, and morality. Franklin said,

> By this means he turned our attention to what was good, just, and prudent in the conduct of life; and little or no notice was taken of what related to the victuals on the table, whether it was ill or well dressed, in or out of season, of good or bad flavor, . . . so that I was brought up with such a perfect inattention to these matters as to be quite indifferent to what kind of food was set before me.[3]

Early Preparation for the Ministry

Josiah and Abiah's faith had consequences for their children. They made sure they were in church each week, and Josiah decided to give his youngest son, Benjamin, as the tithe of his sons to the service of the church. So to prepare him for ministry, he enrolled him in grammar school instead of putting him in an apprenticeship, where he would learn a trade. His Uncle Benjamin approved and promised to loan young Benjamin his volumes of sermons that were written in shorthand, provided he would learn shorthand.

The plan was short-lived, however, because the burden of a large family meant that Josiah was unable to continue to pay for his son's education. So, at the age of ten, Benjamin's formal education ended and he went to work in his father's candle-making and soap-boiling business.

An avid reader and eager student, Benjamin did not let the change dampen his desire to learn. Unusually bright, he could not remember a time when he could not read. And he read voraciously everything he could get his hands on.

When Benjamin had his own money, his first purchase of books was "separate little volumes" of John Bunyan's works. Bunyan (1628-1688) was the famous Puritan preacher who spent time in an English prison for his faith and who wrote the classic, *Pilgrim's Progress*. He once referred to Bunyan as "my favorite author."

He Learns the Printing Business

Seeing that Benjamin had such a passion for books, his father decided that he should be a printer. So he arranged an apprenticeship for him with his older brother, James, who owned a printing business in Boston.

The arrangement required that Benjamin sign an agreement that made him, in reality, an indentured servant to his brother. He was 12 years old at the time. The agreement required that he work as an apprentice with his brother until he was 21 and that, during the final year, he would receive journeyman's wages.

Benjamin liked the exposure to the vast array of books that were being printed and sold. Sometimes, he would borrow a book, spend most of the night reading it, and then return it in the morning.

In 1721, James began publishing a newspaper, *The New England Courant*, which was only the second—or perhaps, the third—newspaper in America. He invited some of his friends to write short pieces for the paper, thus increasing its circulation and its popularity.

When Benjamin had an urge to write a piece, he perceived that James would reject it, since he was so young. Nevertheless, he secretly wrote a piece anonymously and slipped it under the newspaper office door at night. The next day, when James and his friends read the piece, they liked it, published it, and tried to guess who the author might be. With such affirmation, he continued to slip anonymous editorials under the door at night.

Finally, he was discovered. James, rather than commending him, rebuked him and stopped publishing Benjamin's writings. His reason? It would make him vain! Arguments increased and tensions mounted, until one day, Benjamin ran away to Philadelphia, about 300 miles to the south.

During the period of tension, James had beat him physically on several occasions. Reflecting later on this, Benjamin wrote,

> Perhaps the harsh and tyrannical treatment of me was a means of impressing me with the aversion to arbitrary power that has stuck to me through my whole life.[4]

He Separates from His Brother

During this period, a series of events occurred, which led to the shortening of his apprenticeship period so that, when he left, it was without breaking the original, formal agreement. It began when his brother printed a political piece that offended the Assembly, the governing body of the Massachusetts Bay Colony. When James would not reveal the author of the piece, the Assembly imprisoned him for a month. Despite the ill will between him and James, Benjamin resented the Assemblies actions.

With James in prison, Benjamin took responsibility for the print shop and the publication of the newspaper. Because of his depth of knowledge, his ability to write, and his quick wit, he was able, he says, "to give our rulers some rubs, which my brother took very kindly." Others were not so pleased, considering him a brash youth with an inclination for libeling and satire.

When James was released from prison, his discharge included an order preventing him from any longer printing *The New England Courant*. After consultation, James decided to continue printing the paper, but using his brother's name, Benjamin Franklin. In order to remove the possibility of being charged with publishing the paper through his apprentice, he had to cancel the indentured agreement, which freed Benjamin from that legal obligation.

After several months of the paper being published under Benjamin's name, a new disagreement arose between the two brothers. In what he later considered a mistake on his part, Benjamin exerted his freedom and left his brother's print shop. There were hard feelings on both sides. His brother spread a negative report about Benjamin to all of the other printers in town, thus preventing him from future employment in the printing industry in Boston.

He Runs Away to Philadelphia

In addition, realizing that he had created bad feelings with the politicians through his writings, he decided it was time to leave Boston. By now, Benjamin was 17.

To scrape together enough money to travel, he sold his precious books. And knowing that his parents would stop him if they discovered his plan to leave, he secretly arranged with a friend to board a sloop in Boston Harbor and sail to New York.

Three days later, he arrived in New York City "without the least recommendation, or knowledge of any person in the place, and very little money in my pocket."

He found a printer and applied for employment. Although the shop owner, Mr. Bradford, had no work for him, he recommended that he travel to Philadelphia where his son, also a printer, needed help in his shop. So he boarded a ship for Philadelphia.

It was not an easy journey. The ship ran into stormy weather, and a drunken, fellow passenger added to the misery. When the ship reached its destination, north of Philadelphia, the crew and passengers had to spend the night onboard. As the storm continued through the night, the rain seeped through the hatches, soaking the passengers who were huddled together, trying to sleep.

The next morning, weary and wet, Benjamin set out on foot for the 50-mile journey to Burlington where he would catch another boat to Philadelphia. Finally, on Sunday morning, he arrived at the Market Street Wharf in Philadelphia. It was quite an arrival for a young man who would become, in the minds of many, the city's most famous citizen. Reflecting on his arrival, he wrote,

> I was in my working dress, my best clothes coming around by sea. I was dirty from being so long in the boat. My pockets were stuffed out with shirts and stockings, and I knew no one, nor where to look for lodging. Fatigued with walking, rowing and want of sleep, I was very hungry; and my whole stock of cash consisted in a single dollar and about a shilling in copper coin.[5]

He Thanks God for His Providential Care

In later life, Benjamin would thank God and attribute his success in life to God's providential blessings. When he was nearly 70, he included this in his *Autobiography*.

> And now as I speak of thanking God, I desire with all humility to acknowledge that I attribute the mentioned happiness of my past life to his divine providence, which led me to the means I used and gave the success. My belief of this induces me to hope that the same goodness will still be exercised toward me; the complexion of my future fortune being known only to him only in whose power it is to bless us, even in our afflictions.[6]

Chapter 2

Carving Out a New Life in Philadelphia

> *I dressed plainly and was seen at no places of idle diversion . . . I spent no time in taverns, games or frolics of any kind.*
> Benjamin Franklin

When Franklin arrived in Philadelphia, it was the colonies' third largest town, with a population of about 12,000. The streets were unpaved, and a visitor from England said it reminded him of the "country market towns in England." It was small, but bustling and growing, and it would eventually surpass both Boston and New York City to become the largest city in Colonial America.

Philadelphia Founded by Christian Reformers

Philadelphia was the capital of Pennsylvania, a colony founded in 1681 by the devout English Quaker, William Penn, who had been imprisoned for his faith in an English prison.

When he was given Pennsylvania by King Charles II as repayment for a debt owed to his father, an admiral in the

British navy, he determined to make Pennsylvania a haven for Quakers and members of other persecuted religious groups. It would function with minimal taxation and regulation, with the people expected to govern themselves from within, according to the law of Christian love and Biblical principles. Penn's maxim was: "He who will not be governed by God must be ruled by tyrants."

Penn founded and named the city of Philadelphia, deriving its name from two New Testament Greek words: *phileo,* meaning "love;" and *adelphos,* meaning "brother." Hence, *Philadelphia,* "City of Brotherly Love." The name expressed his desire that Philadelphia and all of Pennsylvania would be characterized and guided by Christian love.

Quakers were dominant in Philadelphia and throughout Pennsylvania when Franklin arrived. But as was the case with the second and third generation Puritans in New England, many had lost the vision and passion for Christian reform that had brought their parents and grandparents to the New World. Religion still prevailed, but it was tainted by an obvious preoccupation with earthly affairs and a sense of spiritual indifference.

He Finds Lodging and Employment

Hungry and tired, Franklin walked up Market Street and came upon a bakery where he bought three loaves of bread. With a loaf under each arm, he walked up the street, munching on the third. He continued walking and eventually, came across many well-dressed people going in the same direction, and so he decided to follow them.

As it turned out, these were Quakers going to "the great meetinghouse," and he entered and sat down.

The Quakers did not have an appointed leader or written order of service, but they sat in silence until someone felt "moved by the Spirit" to speak. Franklin looked around but not seeing or hearing anyone move or speak, and being drowsy from his grueling journey, he fell off to sleep. He slept through the meeting and might have slept longer, but someone roused him and informed him the meeting was over.

A young Quaker man directed him to a place where he could lodge, and the next day he found the printer, the son of the Mr. Bradford in New York City who had directed him to Philadelphia. Bradford, however, did not need help in his shop, but he directed him to another printer in town, Mr. Keimer. Keimer asked him a few questions about printing, and realizing he had knowledge and experience, hired him as his assistant.

His Social Life & Youthful Indiscretions

Being only 17, he began making friends with other young people, especially those who shared his love for books and learning. They would spend certain appointed times in the evening, reading and discussing various topics and books. They also engaged in writing poetry and prose, and then in critiquing each other's writing. Franklin found this very profitable in helping him improve his writing skills.

In the midst of his interactions with other youth in the city, Franklin had a sexual escapade with a young woman whose name was never revealed. But in 1730, when he was 24, he publicly acknowledged the existence of a son, William, who had been born out of wedlock. Without divulging the identity of the mother, Franklin took William into his home and raised him.

In his *Autobiography*, he describes himself, at this time, as being "under no religious restraint," clearly indicating that "religious restraints" later became a governing, moral force in his life.

Philosophy & Book Clubs Formed

Through his readings, Franklin discovered the Socratic Method of Argumentation. This method was named after the Greek philosopher, Socrates, and involves the posing of questions, rather than direct opposition to another's position. By asking the right questions, one might lead another to contradict himself in some way, thus strengthening his own position.

Franklin became adept at this method and used it in his many discussions with his employer, Keimer, who had some strange religious views and had even considered starting his own religious sect. By asking leading questions, Franklin was often able to surprise Keimer into revealing his own inconsistencies. As a result, Keimer became very cautious of Franklin's questions, and would ask, "What do you intend to infer by that question?"

Motivated by his love of learning and of discussing ideas, Franklin founded *The Junto*, which began with twelve members formed for the purpose of discussing Morals, Politics, or Natural Philosophy. Franklin wrote,

Our debates were to be under the direction of a president, and to be conducted in the sincere inquiry after truth, without fondness for dispute nor desire for victory.[7]

The Junto grew and became influential in the social and political affairs of Philadelphia. Out of it emerged the American Philosophical Society.

The members of The Junto pooled their books so that everyone would have access to the accumulated number. At first, they were kept in one of the member's home, but later, they were moved to the State House, which housed offices and meetings of the governing Assembly. Franklin conceived the idea of making it a subscription library, using the money from subscriptions to purchase more books. The idea was a success and today the library is known as the Library Company of Philadelphia, comprising more than 500,000 rare books, pamphlets and manuscripts.

A Frugal and Disciplined Life

Even as a young man, Benjamin Franklin lived a frugal lifestyle. For example, he ate a simple and inexpensive diet, and for a time, he was a vegetarian. While his co-workers spent much money on beer and wine, Franklin drank only water. As a result, he was able to save money, even when his income was small, and he was able to provide help for his closest friends in their times of need.

He was also a disciplined, industrious, and diligent worker, spending long hours in the shop. A Dr. Baird noted his work ethic and commented,

The industry of that Franklin is superior to anything I ever saw of the kind. I see him at work when I go home from the club, and he is at work again before his neighbors are out of bed.[8]

There is no question that Franklin's work ethic can be attributed to his Puritan heritage. He reflected on the fact that when he was a young boy, his father would often quote to him Proverbs 22:29,

Seest thou a man diligent in his business? He shall stand before kings. He shall not stand before mean [insignificant] men (KJV).

His diligence and honest dealings caught the attention of several older, well-established citizens of Philadelphia, who underwrote him in his own printing business while he was still young. His work ethic and integrity gave them confidence to put their own money at risk, and they were not disappointed.

Franklin said that, in order to gain the confidence of creditors to underwrite his printing business, he was careful, not only to be frugal and industrious in fact, but also to avoid even giving an appearance to the contrary. He wrote,

"I dressed plainly and was seen at no places of idle diversion . . . I spent no time in taverns, games or frolics of any kind."[9]

Later in life, Franklin commented on the effect one's work ethic has on creditors, saying,

The most trifling actions that affect a man's credit are to be regarded. The sound of your hammer at five in the morning, or eight at night, heard by a creditor, makes him easy six months longer; but if he sees you at a billiard table, or hears your voice at a tavern, when you should be at work, he sends for his money the next day.[10]

After being set up in his own printing business, Franklin began publishing a newspaper called *The Pennsylvania Gazette*.

Later, he began publishing *Poor Richard's Almanac*, offering a mix of seasonal weather forecasts, information on lunar cycles, practical household hints, puzzles, and other amusements. In it, he sought to teach diligence, frugality, and morality, with witty quips inserted throughout, such as "Early to bed, early to rise, makes a man healthy, wealthy and wise." *The Almanac* generated significant income.

Unquestionably, Franklin inherited his work ethic from his Puritan upbringing. In fact, his detractors have referred to his *Autobiography*, written later in life, as "little else than a Puritan document—a religious tract—for the justification of thrift and other Puritan qualities."[11]

His Marriage to Deborah Reed

In his early days in Philadelphia, Benjamin boarded in the home of a woman who had a daughter named Deborah. Franklin developed a close friendship with her and proposed marriage, but her mother thought it was premature, since she was only eighteen years old. Additionally, Franklin was about to make a trip to England. So Deborah's mother insisted that, if there were to be a wedding, it should occur after his return from England.

26

Franklin had anticipated a brief visit, but it turned into an unexpected eighteen month absence. During that time, he wrote to Deborah only once, something he would later regret. With his extended absence and thinking he might never return, Deborah was persuaded by some of her friends to marry a potter named Rogers. Franklin later described him as a "worthless fellow."

Her marriage to Rogers was short-lived, and when it was rumored that Rogers had another wife, Deborah refused to live with him or to bear his name. In the meantime, he fell into debt, and to escape the wrath of his creditors, he fled to the West Indies, taking Deborah's inheritance with him. It was later reported that he had died in Barbados. This occurred two years after Franklin's return from England.

With Rogers' apparent demise, Franklin renewed his friendship with Deborah, and there was an obvious mutual affection. However, with laws against bigamy and with no actual written proof of Rogers' death, there was much opposition to them being married and many considered such a marriage to be invalid. There was also the possibility that Rogers' debtors would require payment. Franklin wrote,

> We ventured, however, over all these difficulties, and I took her to wife, September 1st, 1730. None of the inconveniences happened that we apprehended; she proved a good and faithful helpmate, assisted me much by attending to the shop; we throve together, and ever mutually endeavored to make each other happy. Thus I corrected that great *erratum* as best I could.

His Attempt at Moral Perfection

About this time, Franklin set out on the "bold and adventurous" project of arriving at moral perfection. He said,

> As I knew, or thought I knew, what was right and wrong, I did not see why I might not always do the one and avoid the other.

To carry out this plan, he created a list of 12 virtues, and each week, he would focus on one, seeking to nurture and develop that particular virtue in his life. His list of virtues included: temperance, silence, order, resolution, frugality, industry, sincerity, justice, moderation, cleanliness, tranquility, and chastity.

He added a thirteenth virtue when a Quaker friend informed him that he was generally considered proud, and he pointed out examples to make his point. So Franklin added "humility" to his list of virtues and determined to make Jesus and Socrates his models for the pursuit of humility.

With this pursuit, he soon realized that he had taken on a more difficult task than he had supposed. He said,

"While my attention was taken up and employed in guarding against one fault, I was often surprised by another."

He finally concluded that the key was to break established bad habits and to replace them with virtuous habits, which would take time.

Reflecting on this endeavor in his 79th year, he wrote,

Though I never arrived at the perfection I was so ambitious of obtaining, but fell far short of it, yet I was, by the endeavor, a better and happier man than I otherwise should have been if I had not attempted it.[12]

His Brief Love Affair with Deism

As a young man, Franklin encountered Deism while reading books by authors who opposed Deism and who quoted their tenets in refuting them. He thought the arguments of the Deists had merit, and he later read books by proponents of Deism. In time, he embraced the Deist arguments and openly declared himself to be a Deist.

Eighteenth century Deists professed to believe in an unknown God who created the universe, established it to function on natural laws, and then left it to run on its own, much like a clockmaker who makes a clock, winds it up, and then leaves it to run on its own. Some have described the God of the Deist as acting like an absent landlord.

Deists denied Scripture, claiming it to be a faulty, inadequate resource for truth, and instead they emphasized human logic and reason as the paths to knowledge and truth. They denied the deity of Christ and other orthodox Christian doctrines. Further, they claimed that, since God is not involved in His creation, there are no such things as miracles or answers to prayer and there are no rewards or punishment for behavior.

Evidence points to the fact that Franklin moved away from Deism as he matured. In his *Autobiography*, he recounts how his arguments for Deism had perverted some of his young acquaintances. In hindsight, he viewed his influence on these young friends, not as a "conversion," but as a "perversion" of their thinking.[13]

His commitment to pure Deistic thinking was brief because he saw the unsavory results of such a belief system. When he considered the wrongs that others had inflicted on him, and the wrongs he had inflicted on his wife, he realized that a moral compass was necessary to influence behavior and that Deism did not provide this. He decided that, because Deism offered no rewards or punishments to motivate human behavior, then even if true, it was not very useful.

So, at a young age, Franklin formulated his own creed. He derived it from his knowledge and experience at the time, and it clearly shows that he had already moved away from some of the basic tenets of Deism. Here are the tenets of his belief system:

1. There is one God who made all things.

2. He governs the world by His providence.

3. He ought to be worshipped by adoration, prayer and thanksgiving.

4. The most acceptable service to God is doing good to man.

5. The soul is immortal.

6. God will certainly reward virtue and punish vice, either here or hereafter.[14]

Franklin's shift away from Deism was not difficult, perhaps in part, because it was not inherent in his upbringing. At this point, he was negotiating life with a thoughtful pursuit of truth, and there would come into his life a person who would further influence him toward historic Christianity. That person was George Whitefield.

George Whitefield (1714-1770), the most famous preacher of the Great Awakening (1726-1770), would become Franklin's close friend and business partner and would significantly impact his view of God, church, and human existence.

A New Friend and the Great Awakening

> *It was wonderful to see the change soon made in the manners of our inhabitants. From being thoughtless or indifferent about religion, it seemed as if all the world were growing religious.*
> Benjamin Franklin

George Whitefield was a graduate of Oxford University, where he had come under the influence of the Wesley brothers, John (1703-1791) and Charles (1707-1788). At Oxford, he became a part of the Holy Club, a pietistic group of devout students, which later morphed into the Methodist Revival. After graduation, he was ordained with the Anglican Church at the age of 21, and when Dr. Benson, Bishop of Gloucester, laid hands on him, he recalled,

"My heart was melted down, and I offered up my whole spirit, soul and body, to the service of God's sanctuary."[15]

Being a gifted orator and a passionate preacher, he soon made a name for himself as "The Boy Preacher." Huge crowds gathered, both in churches and outdoors, to hear him preach in and around London. With the Wesleys, he spearheaded the Methodist Revival in Great Britain.

In 1739, sensing a divine call to America, the 24-year- old Whitefield sailed from England with the prayer that God would forge the scattered American colonists into "one nation under God."

He arrived in Philadelphia in the fall of 1739, and his preaching had an immediate and profound impact on the city. No building in Philadelphia was large enough to accommodate the thousands who flocked to hear him preach, and he was forced to preach outdoors. The meetings were nonsectarian, and in his *Autobiography* Franklin wrote,

> In 1739 there arrived among us from Ireland the Reverend Mr. Whitfield who made himself remarkable there as an itinerant preacher. He was at first permitted to preach in some of our churches, but the clergy, taking a dislike to him, soon refused him their pulpits, and he was obliged to preach in the fields. The multitudes of all sects and denominations that attended his sermons were enormous, and it was a matter of speculation to me, who was one of the number, to observe the extraordinary influence of his oratory on his hearers. It was wonderful to see the change soon made in the manners of our inhabitants. From being thoughtless or indifferent about religion, it seemed as if all the world were growing religious so that one could not walk through the town in an evening without hearing psalms sung in different families of every street.[16]

Franklin was obviously thrilled at what he saw, and he considered the revival a positive influence on the city. In fact, he describes the transformation of the manners of the people as "wonderful." There is not the slightest hint of any concern or hesitation from Franklin concerning this Great Awakening.

Whitefield Fans the Flame of the "Great Awakening"

Whitefield emphasized that church membership, good works, family pedigree, and position in life were of no value in making one acceptable to God. He pointed out that these were "faulty foundations" upon which many had put their trust. What was necessary, Whitefield preached, was a new birth through faith in Jesus Christ.

Although accounts of his meetings often describe the multitudes as standing and listening in rapt silence, accounts also reveal intense emotional responses experienced at times to his preaching, as well as spiritual manifestations, such as weeping, falling and crying aloud to God. On one occasion, after preaching to a huge throng gathered outdoors, Whitfield surveyed the crowd and noted the amazing response.

> Look where I would, most were drowned in tears. Some were struck pale as death, others wringing their hands, others lying on the ground, others sinking into the arms of their friends and most lifting up their eyes to heaven and crying out to God.

The "Great Awakening," as it came to be known, spread up and down the eastern seaboard, thanks in great part to Whitefield's untiring labors and nonstop travels. Everywhere he went, huge crowds turned out to hear him preach. In Boston, a massive crowd, that some estimated at 25,000—more than the population of the city—gathered on Boston Common to hear him preach. He became the most recognizable figure in Colonial America, as a result.

In his *Autobiography*, Franklin admits that he was skeptical of reports of Whitefield's preaching being heard by crowds of 25,000 and more. So, with his enquiring, scientific mind, he devised a way to settle it for himself. On one occasion, while Whitefield was preaching to a huge crowd from the top of the Philadelphia Courthouse steps, Franklin stepped off the distance to which Whitefield's voice could be heard.

> Imagining then a semi-circle of which my distance would be the radius, and that it was filled with auditors, to each of whom I allowed two square feet, I computed that he might well be heard by more than thirty thousand. This reconciled me to the newspaper reports of his having preached to twenty-five thousand people in the fields.[17]

Franklin's Friendship with Whitefield

Whitefield visited Philadelphia many times. On his first visit, he was introduced to Franklin who was eight years his senior. This proved to be the beginning of a close friendship that lasted until Whitefield's death 31 years later. At times during those years, Whitefield stayed in Franklin's home when visiting Philadelphia.

Franklin, the businessman, devised an arrangement to print and distribute Whitefield's sermons and journals. It was a win-win deal, providing increased business and income for Franklin, while allowing Whitefield to expand his influence through the printed page.

The demand for Whitefield's sermons and journals was great. The May 22, 1740, edition of *The Pennsylvania Gazette* carried this notice:

> The whole number of names subscribed far exceeds the number of books printed. Those subscribers who have paid or who bring the money in their hands will have preference.

Whitefield sought Franklin's advice in business matters related to his ministry, not only concerning the printing and distribution of his sermons, but also concerning the establishment of an orphanage in Georgia. In this regard, Franklin tells a humorous, personal story to illustrate the power of Whitefield's preaching.

Franklin had advised Whitefield to bring the orphans to Philadelphia and to build the orphanage there instead of putting out the extra expense involved in shipping building materials to Georgia. Whitefield rejected this advice, and so Franklin decided he would not contribute to the project.

Not too long after this decision, Franklin was attending one of Whitefield's outdoor meetings. Toward the end of the sermon, he perceived that Whitefield was about to receive an offering for the orphanage. He said,

"I silently resolved he should get nothing from me."

His resolve, however, wilted under Whitefield's preaching, and he wrote,

> I had in my pocket a handful of copper money, three or four silver dollars, and five pistoles in gold. As he proceeded I began to soften, and concluded to give the copper. Another stroke of his oratory made me ashamed of that, and determined me to give the silver; and he finished so admirably that I emptied my pocket wholly into the collector's dish, gold and all.[18]

Whitefield had his critics, who, among other things, suggested that he used the money collected for the orphanage for his own personal use. In his *Autobiography*, written years after the fact, Franklin came to his defense and wrote,

> I, who was intimately acquainted with him, being employed in printing his Sermons and Journals, never had the least suspicion of his integrity, but am to this day decidedly of opinion that he was in all his conduct a perfectly honest man.[19]

Whitefield made seven visits to America and always spent time with his printer friend in Philadelphia. Before one of his visits, he wrote Franklin a letter informing him that his normal place of lodging in Philadelphia was not available because his host had moved from Philadelphia to Germantown. Franklin heartily welcomed him to stay in his home, and the evidence indicates that Franklin's home became Whitefield's home when he was in Philadelphia.

Whitefield's biographer, Thomas S. Kidd, has pointed out that, during his second visit to Philadelphia, Whitefield preached some very pointed and searching sermons against Deism, perceiving that Philadelphia was "a stronghold of Deism."[20] It obviously did not affect his friendship with Franklin. Perhaps, at this time, Franklin was no longer so closely identified with Deism, as to take it personally. Perhaps, he considered Whitefield's argument to have merit.

Whatever the case in that regard, their friendship deepened. Whitefield continued to seek Franklin's advice in matters of business, and Franklin continued to publish Whitefield's sermons and journals. They continued to correspond, and Franklin once said to his brother James,

"Whitefield is a good man and I love him."

Whitefield was not shy in urging Franklin to embrace the New Birth and evangelical faith. Franklin was not offended, and he would respond congenially, often thanking Whitefield for his prayers. In one letter to Whitefield, seeking to assuage his concerns, Franklin expressed confidence that God loved him and added,

"And if He loves me can I doubt that He will go on to take care of me, not only here but hereafter?"[21]

Franklin Returns to His Puritan Roots

In his *Autobiography*, written several years after Whitefield's death, Franklin says that Whitefield often prayed for his conversion, but that he did not live to see his prayers answered. Nonetheless, there is no question that Whitefield's influence moved Franklin back toward his Puritan roots of faith and freedom.

This was already apparent a few years after Whitefield's initial visit. Britain and Spain were at war, and the people of Philadelphia were concerned about their safety because Britain was providing no protection. Spanish ships could move in at any moment.

Being the leader that he was, Franklin organized a citizens' militia and the building of fortifications with cannons at the edge of the city. He then proposed that the Assembly and civic leaders issue a call for a day of prayer and fasting, "to implore the blessing of Heaven on our undertaking."

The idea of a public day of prayer and fasting was foreign to the people of Philadelphia. But, Franklin, drew on his Puritan roots in New England, where public days of prayer and fasting had been observed since the time the Pilgrims landing at Plymouth in 1620. He wrote,

> They embraced the motion; but as it was the first fast ever thought of in the province, the secretary had no precedent from which to draw the proclamation. My education in New England, where a fast is proclaimed every year, was here of some advantage. I drew it in the accustomed style, it was translated into German, printed in both languages, and divulged through the province.[22]

Franklin and all of Pennsylvania, including government officials, participated in this day of prayer and fasting, imploring God's blessing and protection on their colony. Even at this relatively early stage in life, he obviously saw

39

no conflict between God, prayer, and government. Indeed, throughout his life, Franklin would consider Christian values a necessary force for a prosperous and stable society.

His Vision for a Christian Nation

There is no question that, through Whitefield's friendship, Franklin moved toward an evangelical Christian faith in his thinking. Perhaps in his own unique way, he became an orthodox Christian.

In 1756, Franklin proposed that he and Whitefield partner to establish a new colony in Ohio that would honor God and advance the Christian faith. He wrote,

> I imagine we could do it effectually and without putting the nation at too much expense. What a glorious thing it would be, to settle in that fine country a large strong body of religious and industrious people! What a security to the other colonies; and advantage to Britain, by increasing her people, territory, strength and commerce. Might it not greatly facilitate the introduction of pure religion among the heathen, if we could, by such a colony, show them a better sample of Christians than they commonly see in our Indian traders, the most vicious and abandoned wretches of our nation?[23]

Comparing his life to a drama and himself in the "final act," Franklin explained that he would like to "finish handsomely" by giving himself to such a project. "In such an enterprise," he said, "I could finish my life with pleasure, and I firmly believe God would bless us with success."

Commenting on Franklin's proposal, historian, Thomas S. Kidd, wrote,

> The printer may have doubted some specifics of Christian doctrine, but he hardly questioned the merit of working for God's honor and the public good.[24]

Franklin's proposal was, in fact, far more significant than this. It demonstrates, again, that Franklin saw no conflict between faith and public affairs. It reiterates the fact that he considered Christianity necessary for a healthy and stable society.

That he wanted Whitefield to partner with him in this venture demonstrates his high regard for Whitefield, as well as his personal commitment to the evangelical-revivalism preached by his friend. He refers to Whitefield's approach as "pure religion."

It should also be noted that Franklin's proposal clearly resonates with the founding documents of the earliest Puritan communities of New England, which gave honor to God and expressed a desire to spread the Christian faith. For example, in the Mayflower Compact (signed on November 11, 1620), the Pilgrims, stated that they had come to America, "for the glory of God and the advancement of the Christian faith."

Another example of such a desire is John Winthrop, who founded Boston in 1630 with a company of Puritan families. He envisioned a Christian "commonwealth" or nation, and he expressed his desire that they be that shining "City on a Hill," spoken of by Jesus in Matthew 5:14. He wanted to demonstrate a better example of Christianity than was then seen in England and Europe.

Franklin would have been intimately acquainted with these efforts, and his proposal indicates a return to his Puritan roots in his thinking, as well as his affinity with the vision of his forebears for a Christian nation.

Whitefield may actually have played a role in fostering this perspective in Franklin. When he preached in Boston and other New England towns, he implored the people to return to the faith of their Puritan forebears, and Franklin would have read and printed these passionate entreaties.

Due to time, distance, and various circumstances, the specific venture was not executed. But, I would suggest that Franklin's vision of a Christian colony did not die, but, in fact, was fulfilled on a much larger scale, beyond what he could have imagined. It was twenty years after the date of the original proposal that Franklin, along with 55 others, signed the Declaration of Independence, bringing into existence a new nation—one built on Christian values of faith and freedom.

Friends to the Very End

Whitefield must have noticed the transformation in Franklin's thinking, but lacking a clear public confession of faith from his friend, he carried a concern for Franklin's conversion until his own passing in 1770. Two years earlier, Whitfield had written to Franklin, reminding him,

You and I shall soon go out of the world—ere long we shall see it burnt—Angels shall summon us to attend on the funeral of time—And (oh transporting thought) we shall see eternity rising out of its ashes. That you and I may be in the happy number of those in the midst of the tremendous final blaze and shall cry Amen—Hallelujah—is my hearty prayer.[25]

A brief, two years later, during his seventh visit to America, Whitefield passed away. He had been continuing his incessant travels and preaching, despite coughing blood, chest pains, and overall physical weakness. The end was near.

He was preaching near Newburyport, Massachusetts, when he retired to spend the night at the home of his friend, Reverend Jonathan Parsons. He spent a restless night, awakening at one point with trouble breathing. Nonetheless, he was able to muse about whether to winter in Boston or in the South. Eventually, he went back to sleep, only to awaken later with tightness in his chest and difficulty breathing. Finally, he stopped breathing altogether, and despite a doctor's attempts to revive him, he left this earth at 6 A.M. on September 30, 1770.

Offers to bury him came from New Hampshire and from Boston's Old South Church, but Parsons quickly arranged for Whitefield's interment in the vault of the Newburyport Presbyterian Church. The funeral service included a prayer by Daniel Rogers, a loyal friend who had been converted under Whitefield's ministry thirty years earlier. He said that "he owed his conversion to the labors of that dear man of God, whose precious remains now lay before them." Rogers then began weeping and crying, "O my father, my father!" The congregation melted into tears. [26]

Condolences poured in from throughout the colonies and from Great Britain. Franklin was visiting London at the time of Whitefield's death, and when he received word of his friend's passing, he wrote,

> I knew him intimately upwards of thirty years; his integrity, disinterestedness, and indefatigable zeal in prosecuting every good work, I have never seen equaled, I shall never see exceeded.[27]

Benjamin Franklin was never the same as a result of his close friendship with George Whitefield, the most famous preacher of the Great Awakening.

He Gains Social
and Political Influence

> *Do you see a person diligent in their business?*
> *They shall stand before kings; they shall not stand*
> *before mean [insignificant] people*
> Proverbs 22:29

In his *Autobiography*, Franklin tells how, in his childhood, his father would often quote Proverbs 22:29 to him. He grew up understanding it to be an exhortation that diligence is a strategic means of obtaining prosperity, and he sought to apply this trait personally. He added that he had seen the passage literally fulfilled beyond anything he could have imagined: he had had meetings with five different kings and he had dined with two.

By 1747, Franklin had accumulated enough wealth that he was able to retire from the printing business. He did not completely withdraw, but created a partnership with his foreman, David Hall, an arrangement that afforded him half of the shop's profits. He also continued writing for *Poor Richard's Almanac*. Also, by this time, he had other sources of income and was able to give himself to his scientific pursuits, as well as to reading, education, and politics.

The emerging science of electricity intrigued him, and he began his own experiments. He was, in fact, the first to identify the positive and negative electrical currents and, with his famous kite experiment, he proved that lightening is electricity. He also invented such devices as bifocals and the popular Franklin stove, which produced more heat at less expense. His scientific experiments and inventions gained him renown in both America and Great Britain.

This brought him recognition by major universities. In 1762, Oxford University awarded him an honorary doctorate, and from then on, he was commonly referred to as "Dr. Franklin." Harvard and Yale also awarded him honorary doctorates.

His Reputation and Influence Grow

Especially beginning in 1748, Franklin's influence increased. That year, he was selected as a Philadelphia city councilman, and in 1751, he was elected a member of the Assembly, the governing body for Pennsylvania. Hearing of his diligence and honesty, the British government hired him to be the Postmaster-General for North America. He took on the task with characteristic enthusiasm, overhauling the mail system, creating a more efficient and profitable enterprise.

In 1764, he was elected speaker of the Assembly. Shortly thereafter, he was chosen to go to England to represent the concerns of the colonists regarding the Stamp Act. This had been passed by the British Parliament on March 22, 1765, requiring all American colonists to pay taxes on every piece of paper they printed, including, for example: legal documents, licenses, newspapers, other publications, and even such items as playing cards.

While in England on this government business trip, he met with Whitefield in London. The two had a pleasant time, reminiscing, catching up, and discussing future plans for Whitefield's orphanage in Georgia. Whitefield also attended Franklin's testimony before the British House of Commons on February 13, 1766.

One month later, the Stamp Act was repealed. Whitefield wrote in his journal, "Stamp Act repealed, *Gloria Deo*."

In Philadelphia, *The Pennsylvania Gazette* published a letter from "an eminent clergyman in London," believed to have been Whitefield, assuring the readers,

"Dr. Franklin spoke very heartily and judiciously, in his country's behalf."[28]

Founds the University of Pennsylvania as a Christian School

In the fall of 1749, Franklin made known his vision for a school designed "for the education of youth in Pennsylvania." It was established as "The Public Academy of Philadelphia," and it was underwritten with public funds. A unique characteristic of this school was that it would teach, not only the basic rudiments of science, religion, and history, but also practical skills for making a living. In this sense, this was a forerunner of modern vocational schools.

Franklin wrote to Whitefield and shared with him the proposal for the school, noting that the students would learn the value of public and private religion, and the "excellency of the Christian religion above all others." Whitefield, being aware of his friend's previous association with Deism, continued to point him to Jesus, and he did so, again, in this situation. He responded in a letter, commending Franklin for his endeavor, but declaring,

"There wants *aliquid Christi* [something of Christ] to make it so useful as I desire."[29]

How much Franklin responded to Whitefield's input concerning the school is not clear, but it certainly did not hinder their friendship, since it was after this that Franklin proposed that they establish a Christian colony "on the Ohio." For his part, Franklin was already committed to the teaching of Christian and Biblical values, which he believed necessary for a prosperous and stable society.

Franklin wanted Christian principles to be taught in the school, but not in a sectarian manner. To accommodate this, he arranged for the different Christian denominations to be represented equally on the Board of Trustees, choosing one Anglican, one Presbyterian, one Baptist, one Moravian, one Quaker, and so on, to serve.

Showing his desire for a profound Christian influence in the school, he handpicked the first Provost from the clergy, a Reverend William Smith. To house the school, he acquired a large building, built some years earlier to accommodate the large crowds that had turned out to hear George Whitefield. Franklin negotiated a favorable settlement, which included an agreement that the school would "keep forever open in the building a large hall for occasional preachers, according to the original intention."[30]

The Academy flourished and today it is the University of Pennsylvania.

He Opposes the Deism of Thomas Paine

Franklin, indeed, came to believe the teachings of Jesus— whom he sought to emulate—to be a necessary and positive force in society and a restraint against evil in the world. This is why, when the well-known Deist, Thomas Paine, sent him a manuscript copy of a book he had written, challenging the idea of a providential God and other aspects of orthodox Christianity, Franklin, in very strong language, urged him not to print the book or even allow anyone else to see it. He wrote,

> I would advise you, therefore ... to burn this piece before it is seen by any other person; whereby you will save yourself a great deal of mortification by the enemies it may raise against you, and perhaps a good deal of regret and repentance. If men are so wicked with religion [Christianity], what would they be if without it.[31]

Nevertheless, Paine published *The Age of Reason,* which became popular in America. Franklin's words predicting regret and repentance for Thomas Paine, if he persisted in attacking Christianity proved to be prophetic. Years later, on his deathbed in England, Paine expressed deep regret for writing and publishing the book. While in the throes of death, he lamented,

> I would give worlds, if I had them, if *The Age of Reason* had never been published. O Lord, help me! Christ, help me! Stay with me! It is hell to be left alone.[32]

Franklin, the Presbyterian

Franklin was a member of the Presbyterian Church in Philadelphia. Why Presbyterian? The answer becomes clear in historical context.

Presbyterianism was, in Scotland, the counterpart of Puritanism in England. Both were Christian reform movements that advocated for religious liberty and opposed the controlling structure and policies of the official state church, The Church of England.

Philadelphia had no Puritan churches, but Presbyterians from Scotland and Ireland had immigrated to the Middle Colonies, with some settling in Philadelphia. Franklin would have been attracted to Presbyterianism because of the similarities with the Puritanism in which he had been reared.

In fact, the popular Westminster Confession was a joint Statement of Faith formulated by Puritans and Presbyterians who had convened at Westminster in opposition to the oppressive policies of Charles I against both groups. It affirmed Protestant beliefs, such as the ultimate authority of the Bible. It also discussed the relationship between church and state, declaring the right of the people to resist tyrannical rulers, both civil and religious. In addition, it contained the Lord's Prayer and the Apostles Creed.

Next to the Bible, the Westminster Confession became the most widely read piece of literature in Colonial America. Assent to it was required for entry into Harvard, Yale, and the College of New Jersey, now Princeton. In 1745, Franklin began publishing an edition of the Confession, and this action contributed to his wealth. That he assented to the contents of the document is affirmed by the fact that in a letter to a young admirer he exhorted, "Don't forget your catechism," a reference to the Westminster Confession.[33]

Although a life-long member of the Presbyterian Church in Philadelphia, Franklin stopped attending when Reverend Hemphill, a young man who had become the congregation's minister in 1734 was dismissed. Franklin was impressed with the practicality of his preaching, as well as his animated delivery and became "one of his constant hearers."

When some of the elders brought ambiguous charges against him about areas of doctrine, Franklin became his most vocal defender. But Hemphill came under further criticism when his critics discovered that he had borrowed a sermon from a Dr. Foster without revealing his source, causing many of his supporters to abandon him, and he was dismissed.

Franklin was disgusted with the proceedings and stopped attending the services, although he continued to pay his subscription to the church until the time of his death.

In regards to the charge against Hemphill of preaching another's sermons, Franklin wittingly replied,

"I rather approved his giving us good sermons composed by others, than bad ones of his own manufacture."

It was after this event that Franklin met Whitefield.

Separating from Church, Not from God

For the Protestant, including Benjamin Franklin, separating from church did not equal separating from God. From the time of Luther, Protestants had taught the priesthood of all believers, meaning that a Christian has direct access to God through Jesus Christ, apart from the mediation of a priest, minister, or religious institution.

The Pilgrims who landed at Plymouth in 1620 were "separatist" Puritans in that they had separated from the official state church. They had not separated themselves from God, however, and were on a mission to discover a more pure and Biblical form of church and worship.

This is why, when Whitefield was denied access to many of the churches during his initial visit to the Colonies, he was not fazed, and was content to preach in the open fields. Church, for Whitefield, did not equal God. No doubt, this was an area where Franklin felt a deep affinity with Whitefield. Church and God were not synonymous in the thinking of either man.

This distinction is important in understanding the thinking of the Founders in church-state matters. Although they wanted a separation of church and state, there is no evidence whatsoever that they wanted a separation of God and state. On the contrary, the evidence overwhelmingly demonstrates that they saw the necessity of Christian principles and values for both a free and a stable society. This is why John Adams said,

> Our Constitution was made only for a moral and religious people. It is wholly inadequate for the government of any other.[34]

Franklin Lives as a Christian

Although Franklin stopped attending the Presbyterian Church in his hometown, he heartily attended other religious gatherings, such as the meetings of Whitefield. And when he learned that his daughter had stopped attending church because of a personal dislike for the minister, Franklin wrote a letter in which he exhorted her on "the necessity and duty of attending church." In regards to her not liking the minister, Franklin, with typical wit, reminded her that "pure water is often found to have come through very dirty earth."[35]

Franklin was an avid reader of the Bible and would often quote Scripture in his writings and conversations. He also kept certain Christian events and festivals, including Lent. He spoke of being a vegetarian for a time, saying he had found it to be helpful to his health, and that he celebrated Lent by going back to his vegetarian diet. He wrote, "I have since kept several Lents most strictly, leaving the common diet for that."[36]

After a voyage to England in 1757, during which the ship almost crashed into a small, rocky island in the Atlantic at midnight, the first thing Franklin did upon reaching shore was to seek out a church and offer thanksgiving to God. In a letter to his wife, he wrote,

The bell ringing for church, we went thither immediately and with hearts full of gratitude, returned sincere thanks to God for the mercies we had received.

Franklin Would Not Agree with Modern Secularism

Whether Franklin ever embraced all the tenets of orthodox Christianity and became an evangelical Christian is still subject to debate. What is not in question is the fact that Franklin believed Christianity to be a positive force in society, and that he desired its influence to be present in every public venue, including civil government. Franklin would be appalled at modern attempts to remove expressions of Christianity from the public arena.

Final Years and the Forming of a Christian Nation

> *I have lived, sir, a long time and the longer I live,*
> *the more convincing proofs I see of this truth —*
> *that God governs in the affairs of men.*
>
> Benjamin Franklin

The late Harvard professor, Perry Miller, who has been called "a fair minded atheist," was a recognized expert on Puritanism and early American history. Highlighting the impact of the Great Awakening on Colonial America, he once declared,

> The Declaration of Independence of 1776 was a direct result of the preaching of the evangelists of the Great Awakening.

He said this because the Great Awakening was the first national event experienced by the scattered Colonists of various denominational and theological persuasions, and it served to bring a sense of comradery and nationalism. No one was more instrumental in this than Whitefield through his continual travels up and down the Eastern seaboard, with massive crowds gathering everywhere he went. Although he was an ordained Anglican and a leader in

55

the Methodist Revival, he was not sectarian, reaching out to those of all ethnicities and theological persuasions.

This is highlighted in a sermon that he preached outdoors to a massive crowd. During the sermon he mimicked a conversation with Father Abraham who was looking over the banister of heaven at the gathered multitude representing many sects and denominations.

Whitefield cried out,

"Father Abraham, are there any Anglicans in heaven?"

The answer came back,

"No, there are no Anglicans in heaven."

"Father Abraham, are there any Methodists in heaven?"

"No, there are no Methodists in heaven."

"Are there any Presbyterians in heaven?"

"No, there are no Presbyterians here either."

"What about Baptists or Quakers?"

"No, there are none of those here either."

"Father Abraham," cried Whitefield, what kind of people are in heaven?"

The answer came back,

"There are only Christians in heaven; only those who are washed in the blood of the Lamb."

Whitefield then cried out,

"Oh, is that the case? Then God help me, God help us all, to forget having names and to become Christians in deed and in truth!"

Whitefield also reached out to blacks and Native Americans. After addressing African-Americans in the city of Philadelphia, one black woman stated that he must have been in a trance and insisted,

"Jesus Christ must have told him what to speak to the people or else he could not speak as he did."[37]

On another occasion, after preaching and retiring to his lodging, he reported,

"Near 50 Negroes came to give me thanks for what God had done for their souls."

He considered this an answer to prayer and wrote,

"I have been much drawn in prayer for them, and have seen them wrought upon by the word preached."[38]

Although Whitefield never opposed the institution of slavery, his humane and compassionate treatment of blacks helped release anti-slavery sentiments in Colonial America that eventually led to more overt opposition. This is why historian, Benjamin Hart, said,

> Among the most ardent opponents of slavery were ministers, particularly the Puritan and revivalist preachers."[39]

As a result of the Great Awakening, race relations improved and denominational walls came down. For the first time, the Colonists began to see themselves as a single people with one Divine destiny: *One Nation under God,* as Whitfield had prayed. This is why Thomas Kidd, Professor of History at Baylor University, calls Whitefield "America's Spiritual Founding Father."

By Whitefield's seventh and final visit in 1770, much of the former opposition to his ministry had dissipated. According to Hart,

> The true spirit of Christ had dissolved sectarian differences. America considered itself to be a nation of Christians, pure and simple, as Whitefield noted with satisfaction. "Pulpits, hearts and affections," he said, were opened to him and any preacher of whatever denomination who had a true Christian message to share.[40]

Based on solid evidence, we can safely say that Whitefield and his fellow revivalists struck the winning blow for independence, and Franklin and the other Founding Fathers gathered the results. The connection is obvious in the country's founding documents.

The Declaration of Independence Anchors Rights in God

In the midst of Spiritual awakening in the Colonies, England began imposing burdensome taxes and regulations on the Colonists without their participation. *No taxation without representation,* was the cry. When protests, such as the Boston Tea Party, December 16, 1773, erupted, especially in Boston and New England, two British regiments were assigned to occupy Boston. This brought protests from throughout the Colonies. There were further protests when it was rumored that King George planned to send a "bishop" to impose the Anglican faith on the Colonists.

Beginning in 1774, delegates from the Thirteen Colonies began meeting together in a Continental Congress to discuss how to respond. Eventually, they decided to declare their independence from England and form a new nation.

Franklin was a member of a select committee of five chosen to assist Thomas Jefferson in formulating the Declaration of Independence. Franklin offered minor suggestions to Jefferson for the final edition, which was publicly read for the first time in Philadelphia on July 4, 1776.

This founding document anchors individual rights, not in any human institution or government, but in God.

> *We hold these truths to be self-evident that all men [people] are created equal and are endowed by their Creator with certain inalienable rights such as life, liberty and the pursuit of happiness.*

Jefferson, Franklin, and the other Founders saw human rights as having a transcendent source—God Himself. They and their forebears had suffered the loss of rights, their being given and taken at the whim of a monarch, pope, or bishop, and they were determined, in this new nation, to fix rights in a place beyond human reach. Government, they insisted, did not exist to give or take away rights, but to protect those rights already given by God.

Such a society, however, would require a religious [Christian] and moral people. It was understood that a people who did not know how to govern themselves from within by religious and moral principles would turn such freedom into vice and anarchy. This is why all the Founders wanted Christianity taught in every public venue. They wanted a separation of church and state, not a separation of God and state.

The synonym used for God in the Declaration— "Providence"—was commonly used in the 18th century, even by ministers. It was not a generic, impersonal reference to deity, as some have supposed. Even Whitefield often used it in referring to God. "Providence" was a designation that expressed faith in God as the One who is superintending the course of history and overruling, even the actions of evil men, in order to bring about His plan and purpose.

This is why Roger Williams (1603-1683), a devout follower of Christ, after being banished from Massachusetts by the Puritans in 1636, and making his way in the winter to Rhode Island, founded a city there, which he named "Providence." This expressed his faith that God would overrule the wrong that had been done to him and bring about His plan for his life.

The only clergyman to sign the Declaration, Jonathan Witherspoon (1723-1794), preached a sermon entitled "The Dominion of Providence over the Passions of Men" less than two months before signing the document along with Franklin and the other Founders. Witherspoon was a Presbyterian minister and President of the College of New Jersey, now Princeton University. In this sermon on Providence, he emphasized the necessity of believing that God would bring good out of the evil situation of the day—that the ambition of mistaken princes and the cruelty of oppressive rulers would finally promote the glory of God. This is Providence.

The final paragraph of the Declaration shows the faith of the signers, for it expresses their trust in God for His providential protection and support in their momentous act. It reads,

> And for the support of this declaration, with a firm reliance on the protection of Divine Providence, we mutually pledge to each other our Lives, our Fortunes, and our sacred Honor.

After the signing of the document, and knowing that King George III would view their actions as treason, John Hancock exhorted that "we must all hang together." Franklin quipped,

"Yes, if do not all hang together, we will surely all hang separately."

Ambassador to France

From 1776 to 1785, Franklin served as Ambassador to France for the newly-formed United States of America. He achieved great success in that capacity, securing the assistance of the French in the war against England. He was also the chief American negotiator for peace with Great Britain. These negotiations eventually led to the signing of the Treaty of Paris, signed on September 3, 1783, ending the Revolutionary War of Independence.

While in Paris, he advocated for religious tolerance for French Protestants, and his efforts contributed to Louis XVI signing the Edict of Versailles in November 1787, two years after he had departed. This edict effectively nullified the Edict of Fontainebleau, which had denied Protestants civil status and the right to openly practice their faith.

Franklin also served as the Ambassador to Sweden. He negotiated a treaty with the Swedes, even though he never visited the country.

In 1785, he returned home, freed his two slaves, and began to advocate for the abolition of slavery. Two years later, he participated in the formulation of America's Constitution, the most important document after the Declaration of Independence.

His Call to Prayer at the Constitutional Convention

On June 28, 1787, Franklin was a delegate to the Constitutional Convention, which convened in his hometown of Philadelphia. Much regional disagreement had surfaced and the convention was about to be suspended because of unresolved strife and dissension. At this critical moment, Franklin, now 81 years of age, rose to his feet, and addressed the Convention President, George Washington.

> How has it happened, sir, that we have not hitherto once thought of humbly appealing to the Father of lights to illuminate our understandings? In the beginning of the contest with Great Britain, when we were sensible to danger, we had daily prayers in this room for Divine protection. Our prayers, sir, were heard and they were graciously answered. I have lived, sir, a long time and the longer I live, the more convincing proofs I see of this truth—that God governs in the affairs of men. And if a sparrow cannot fall to the ground without

his notice, is it probable that an empire can rise without His aid? We have been assured, sir, in the sacred writings that *except the Lord build the house, they labor in vain that build it.* I firmly believe this. I therefore beg leave to move that, henceforth, prayers imploring the assistance of heaven and its blessing on our deliberation be held in this assembly every morning before we proceed to business.[41]

Although his proposal was not "formally" adopted, there was much response on a personal level because of the respect he had. According to those present, "an atmosphere of reconciliation seemed to settle over the convention hall." Petty grievances and local interests were laid aside, and the delegates went on to complete their task of formulating the American Constitution and Bill of Rights. Whitefield must have smiled down from heaven on his old friend!

No Deism in His Call to Prayer

That it was Franklin who would call the assembly to prayer shows the depth of his Puritan roots and the impact of Whitefield and the Great Awakening on his life and thinking. The words in this call to prayer show how far he had moved away from his earlier Deistic thinking, for Deists did not believe that God "governs in the affairs of men," and prayer would, to them, be futile.

Franklin's call to prayer demonstrates that he wanted trust in God to be a vital part of this new nation, and he considered it necessary for the nation's success. "Is it probable that an empire can rise without His aid?" was his challenging question. In this strategic moment, Franklin is, doubtless, living out the vision for a Christian society that he had shared with Whitefield 31 years earlier.

Franklin's Vision Fulfilled

In 1756, Franklin had proposed to Whitefield that they establish a Christian colony with "a large, strong body of religious and industrious people." Reflecting the missionary vision of his separatist Puritan forebears when they came to America, Franklin spoke of the potential of such a colony, asking,

> Might it not greatly facilitate the introduction of pure religion among the heathen, if we could, by such a colony, show them a better sample of Christians than they commonly see?[42]

He was confident that God would give them success in such a project "if we undertook it with a sincere regard for his honor."

At that time, Franklin mistakenly thought he was in the "final act" of the drama of his life. He explained to Whitefield that he would like to "finish handsomely" by giving himself to such a project. He said,

"In such an enterprise, I could finish my life with pleasure, and I firmly believe God would bless us with success."[43]

I suggest that Franklin's vision for such a Christian colony or society did not die with the fading of that particular project, but that it was, in fact, fulfilled on a much grander scale in the founding of the United States of America.

America Founded as a Christian Nation

That America was considered a Christian nation **is** obvious from the words and actions of the Founders themselves, including Benjamin Franklin. During the Revolutionary War, no less than 15 calls for prayer were issued by the Continental Congress. Franklin, in his call to prayer, reminded the delegates to the Constitutional Convention that, during the war, when their lives were in danger, "we had daily prayers in this room for Divine protection."

The evidence is overwhelming that America was considered a Christian nation for the first 150 years of her existence. Samples of this evidence include statements of a President, a Supreme Court Justice, Congress, and the Supreme Court.

John Adams (1735-1826) was a Boston lawyer and one of the earliest and most active proponents of independence. He served in the Continental Congress and was a signer of the Declaration of Independence. He also served as the nation's first Vice-President under George Washington (1732-1799), and when Washington refused to serve a third term, he was chosen to succeed him as the second President of the new nation.

No one was more aware of the attitudes and sentiments of the Founders than Adams, and he wrote,

"The general principles on which the fathers achieved independence were the general principles of Christianity."

John Marshall (1755-1835) served as Chief Justice of the Supreme Court for almost 35 years from 1801-1835. Many consider him the greatest of Supreme Court Justices, and his decisions helped lay the foundation for U.S. Constitutional law. He once said,

> The American population is entirely Christian, and with us Christianity and religion are identified. It would be strange, indeed, if with such a people, our institutions did not presuppose Christianity, and did not refer to it, and exhibit relations with it.[44]

The U.S. Congress also declared America to be a Christian nation. In 1854, following an extensive, one-year investigation into America's history, the U.S. Congress declared,

> At the time of the adoption of the Constitution and the Amendments, the universal sentiment was that Christianity should be encouraged, but not any one [denomination]. In this age there can be no substitute for Christianity. . . . That was the religion of the founders of the republic, and they expected it to remain the religion of their descendants.[45]

The U.S. Supreme Court, in 1892, completed a 10-year investigation in which thousands of historical documents were investigated concerning the historical roots of the nation. After citing more than sixty historical precedents, the Court concluded:

> There is no dissonance in these declarations. There is a universal language pervading them all, having one meaning; they affirm and reaffirm that this is a religious nation . . . this is a Christian nation.[46]

Franklin's Hope in Resurrection

Benjamin Franklin died on April 17, 1790 at the age of 84, having realized his dream of establishing a Christian colony or nation. He would have considered this a work of Divine Providence, beyond anything he could have conceived.

It is believed that he died of pleurisy, which is inflammation of the lining around the lungs, causing pain and making breathing difficult. He was buried at the Christ Church Cemetery in Philadelphia. It was estimated that approximately 20,000 people attended his funeral.

That Franklin held out hope of a resurrection is expressed in an epitaph he composed for his tombstone, but which was not used. It is found in the Library of Congress and reads:

Here lies the body of B. Franklin, printer.
Like the cover of an old book;
Its contents torn out and stripped of its lettering and gilding,
Lies here, food for worms.
But the work shall not be lost,
For it will, as he believed, appear once more
In a new and more elegant edition
Revised and corrected
By the Author.

No Separation of God and State

> *Congress shall make no law concerning the establishment of religion or hindering the free exercise thereof.*
>
> First Amendment to the Constitution

All of the Founding Fathers, including Benjamin Franklin, wanted a separation of church and state, not a separation of God and state. This is obvious, not only in their words, but also in their actions. For example, after taking the oath of office with his hand on a Bible—not on some Enlightenment text—George Washington and Congress proceeded to St. Paul's Chapel where they participated in a Christian worship service.

Thomas Jefferson, another "nonreligious" Founder, ended all official presidential documents with the words "in the Year of Our Lord Christ," and while President, he attended church services that were held each Sunday in the chambers of the House of Representatives.

Bible verses and expressions of faith abound on the monuments in our nation's capital.

To understand the original intent of the Founders in formulating the First Amendment, it is important to understand their thinking in regards to God, church, and state. Also, it is of utmost importance to note that the Founders did not view "church" as synonymous with "God." In their thinking, disallowing Congress from establishing a national church—which is what the First Amendment is about—in no way restricted God's role in government, public affairs, and their own lives.

To suggest that allowing a student in a public school graduation to mention faith in a valedictory address somehow violates the "establishment clause" of the First Amendment, is preposterous.

It is equally inane to suggest that a cross at a veteran's memorial constitutes an establishment of religion and violates the First Amendment.

This sort of thinking was unknown to Franklin and every other Founder.

Dissenting Protestants & Religious Liberty

Viewing church and God as intricately linked is a Roman Catholic mode, and to a lesser degree, a Lutheran and Anglican way of thinking. The Founders' thinking in this regard had been shaped by the more radical wing of the Protestant Reformation, which drew a clear line of demarcation between obeying God and obeying church officials. This is the wing of Protestantism with which Franklin identified when he spoke of his forebears as being "dissenting Protestants."

These "dissenting Protestants" were the separatist Puritans, Baptists, Quakers, and others who, among other things, opposed the idea of church and state being merged, as had been the case since the time of Constantine (272-337 AD).

The major reformers, such as Luther (1483-1546), Zwingli (1484-1531), and Calvin (1509-1564), maintained the Constantinian/Roman Catholic model of a national church, sanctioned and supported by the state. In Germany, for example, Lutheranism was upheld, and imposed on the populace, by the German princes. In England, Anglicanism was upheld and imposed by the British monarchs. Those who dissented from the "official" form of worship and doctrine were harassed and persecuted.

The dissenting Protestants did not equate God with church. Many of them left the state churches because of their deep faith in God and commitment to His truth. It was these "dissenting Protestants" who developed ideas of religious liberty and freedom of conscience, which they brought to America and further developed on American soil. This is why historian, Benjamin Hart, has said,

> It was Protestants of the most radical stripe, most zealous in their religious convictions (those whom the America Civil Liberties Union would like to see outlawed from the public discourse) who were in fact the greatest proponents of religious liberty as codified in America's governing charter.[47]

Interestingly, today, it is the "progressive secularists" who seem to have no concept of religious liberty or freedom of conscience and who would impose their view of religion and morality on others. It is the political "Left" that would separate God from state and impose their religion of secularism on the American people, with no regard for a person's conscience or religious convictions. Franklin and the Founders called this tyranny.

When the Founders wrote the First Amendment, they did so in light of the persecutions inflicted by oppressive governments and state churches on their godly parents and grandparents.

In his *Autobiography*, Franklin tells how his grandfather, during the reign of Mary Tudor (1516-1558), had an open Bible fastened underneath the cover of a stool. With one of the children watching at the door for civil or religious authorities, he would turn the stool upside down and read the Bible to his family. In case of danger, he would quickly secure the pages and return the stool upright to its place in the corner of the room. The danger was real! During Mary's reign, 288 Protestants were burned at the stake for their faith.

These "dissenting Protestants" were the ones whose ideas of freedom of conscience and religious liberty ultimately triumphed in America, even among Roman Catholics in Maryland and Anglicans in Virginia. One of the signers of the Declaration of Independence, Charles Carrol, was an influential Roman Catholic from Maryland. That his thinking had been impacted by the dissenting Protestants is obvious in his emphasis on salvation being through faith in Jesus Christ alone, rather than through church and sacraments.

Carrol was the last surviving Signer of the Declaration of Independence, and in 1826, New York City requested from him a copy of the document for deposit in the Public Hall. On the 50-Year Anniversary of that momentous event, he complied with their request and appended this comment to the document.

> Grateful to Almighty God for the blessings which, through Jesus Christ our Lord, He has conferred on my beloved country in her emancipation and on myself in permitting me, under circumstances of mercy, to live to the age of eighty-nine years, and to survive the fiftieth year of American independence. I do hereby recommend to the present and future generations the principles of that important document as the best inheritance their ancestors could bequeath to them, and pray that the civil and religious liberties they have secured to my country may be perpetuated to remotest posterity and extended to the whole family of man.[48]

Jefferson Understood the Role of the First Amendment

Virginia was settled by Anglicans, and for a time, the Anglican Church was the official church of that colony and other groups were persecuted. Thomas Jefferson (1743-1826), who was Anglican and a Virginian, led the way in the fight for religious liberty when he came to the defense of certain Baptists who were arrested and imprisoned for preaching in Virginia without a license. His efforts, along with some help from James Madison

(1751-1836), eventually led to Virginia eliminating a state church and offering religious liberty and equal protection to all.

These circumstances and events shed light on Jefferson's letter, written years later while he was president, to a group of Baptists assuring them that, in the new nation, they would not be persecuted as they had been in colonial Virginia and in the Old World. To assure them of this, he pointed them to the First Amendment, which he referred to as a "wall of separation" between church and state. He obviously saw the First Amendment as a unidirectional wall erected to keep the government out of the church, not to keep God out of the government.

This was confirmed by Joseph Story (1779-1845), who served as a Supreme Court Justice for 34 years from 1811-1845. Commenting on the First Amendment, he said:

> We are not to attribute this prohibition of a national religious establishment to an indifference in religion, and especially to Christianity, which none could hold in more reverence than the framers of the Constitution.[49]

A French Sociologist Sees No Separation of God and State

That America's Founders did not remove God from government was obvious to the young French sociologist, Alexis de Tocqueville (1805-1859), who visited America in 1831 to study her institutions. He wanted to see if he could discover the reason for America's rapid rise to power and affluence. In giving an account of his visit and research, he exclaimed,

"The religious atmosphere of the country was the first thing that struck me on arrival in the United States."

He also commented that the means of improving the government were the same means employed in conversion and the advancement of the Christian faith. He concluded that in America,

> From the beginning, politics and religion contracted
> an alliance which has never been dissolved.[50]

It was obvious to Tocqueville that even though there was no national church established by Congress, God had not been removed from the American government, nor from public life. Instead of Christianity diminishing, as many supposed would happen without state support, it actually flourished.

Tocqueville also noted the obvious difference with France's Revolution, where there was a rejection, not only of church, but also of God. Being predominately Roman Catholic, France did not have a sense of distinction between God and church, as did the dissenting Protestants. The French revolutionists, therefore, rejected, not only church, but also God, replacing the God of the Bible with human reason.

The French Declaration of the Rights of Man did not acknowledge human rights as having their source in the Creator, as did the American Declaration, nor did it state that rights are inherent. With no higher moral guide than human reason and experience, the French Revolution soon descended into anarchy, with 20,000 people being executed because they were considered enemies of the new regime. Hart says,

> The French Revolution is a grim example of how people behave when they are unchecked by a sense of religious obligation.[51]

It is no wonder, then, that George Washington warned America to maintain religion [Christianity] and morality in order to preserve political and social stability.

Washington Warned Against Separating God from State

In his Farewell Address after serving two terms as America's first President, George Washington warned the young nation to guard against the very trends that are being embraced and promoted in America today.

> Of all the dispositions and habits which lead to political prosperity, religion and morality are indispensable supports. In vain would that man claim the tribute of patriotism, who should labor to subvert these great pillars of human happiness, these firmest props of the duties of men and citizens. The mere politician, equally with the pious man, ought to respect and to cherish them. And let us with caution indulge the supposition that morality can be maintained without religion. Whatever may be conceded to the influence of refined education on minds of peculiar structure, reason and experience both forbid us to expect that

national morality can prevail in exclusion of religious principle.

Washington says that religion [Christianity] and morality are indispensable supports for political prosperity, and he warned against the supposition that morality could be sustained apart from the influence of Christianity. In other words, he warned against any attempt to separate God from the state—against trying to secularize the American political system. This is why Mark Hall, Professor of Politics at George Fox University, has said:

> America's Founders did not want Congress to establish a national church, and many opposed establishments at the state level as well. Yet they believed, as George Washington declared in his Farewell Address, that of "all the dispositions and habits which lead to political prosperity, religion and morality are indispensable supports." Moreover, almost without exception, they agreed that civic authorities could promote and encourage Christianity and that it was appropriate for elected officials to make religious arguments in the public square. There was virtually no support for contemporary visions of a separation of church and state that would have political leaders avoid religious language and require public spaces to be stripped of religious symbols.[52]

Franklin Knew Nothing of a Separation of God and State

One must ask, given this information about Benjamin Franklin, that if Franklin was one of America's most nonreligious Founders, how would one describe many of America's current politicians? If Franklin was the most nonreligious of the Founders, then, by comparison, it is clear that our nation has left her Christian moorings and is in desperate need of another Spiritual awakening that will help us regain our spiritual equilibrium and facilitate a return to moral sanity.

It is time for all good people who believe in religious liberty to stand against the contemporary assaults on religious liberty that are based on a wrenched and distorted interpretation of the First Amendment. Knowledge is power and based on the knowledge we now have, we can take our stand and let our voices be heard.

We can do so knowing the Founders are standing with us and joining their voices with ours. By their writings they are still speaking and clearly showing their vision for an America based on Judeo-Christian values of religious liberty, morality and freedom of conscience. In this chorus, Benjamin Franklin's voice blends with the rest as he sings the same melody concerning the importance of a Christian nation built on Christian principles and values.

Endnotes

PREFACE

[1] Benjamin Franklin to Whitefield, July 2, 1756, in Leonard W. Labaree, ed., *The Papers of Benjamin Franklin: April 1, 1755 through September 30, 1756* (New Haven, CT, 1963), 6:468-69; cited by Thomas S. Kidd, *George Whitefield:* America's *Spiritual Founding Father* (New Haven: Yale University Press, 2014), 138

CHAPTER 1

[2] Benjamin Franklin, *The Autobiography of Benjamin Franklin* (New York: Airmont, 1965), 14.

[3] Franklin, 17.

[4] Franklin, 26.

[5] Franklin, 31.

[6] Franklin, 10.

CHAPTER 2

[7] Franklin, 64.

[8] Franklin, 66.

[9] Franklin, 70, 77.

[10] Benjamin Hart, *Faith & Freedom* (Dallas: Lewis & Stanley, 1988), 136.

[11] Franklin, 6.

[12] Franklin, 86.

[13] Franklin, 61.

[14] Franklin, 90.

CHAPTER 3

[15] Luke Tyreman, vol. 1 of *The Life of the Rev. George Whitefield* (New York: Anson D. F. Randolph & Co., 1877), 44.

[16] Franklin, 100.

[17] Franklin, 103.

[18] Franklin, 101-02

[19] Franklin, 102.

[20] Thomas S. Kidd, *George Whitefield: America's Spiritual Founding Father* (New Haven: Yale University Press, 2014), 138

[21] Kidd, 236.

[22] Franklin, 108.

[23] Kidd, 211.

[24] Kidd, 211.

[25] Kidd, 253.

[26] Kidd, 251.

[27] Kidd, 253

CHAPTER 4

[28] Kidd, 242.

[29] Kidd, 210.

[30] Franklin, 114.

[31] This letter is in the Library of Congress and is referred to by numerous writers.

[32] Hart, 309.

[33] Gary Amos and Richard Gardiner, *Never Before in History* (Richardson, TX: Foundation for Thought and Ethics, 1998), 26.

[34] Eddie Hyatt, *America's Revival Heritage* (Grapevine, TX: Hyatt, 2010), 20.

[35] Franklin, 79.

[36] Franklin, 42.

CHAPTER 5

[37] Kidd, 114.

[38] Hyatt, 48.

[39] Hart, 330.

[40] Hart, 224.

[41] Hyatt, 65.

[42] Kidd, 211.

[43] Kidd, 213.

[44] Robert Faulkner, *The Jurisprudence of John Marshall* (Westport, CT: Greenwood Press, 1968), 139.

[45] *Reports of Committees of the House of Representatives*, 6, 8-9; quoted by David Barton, *The Role of Pastors and Christians in Civil Government* (Aledo, TX: WallBuilders, 2003), 21.

[46] *Church of the Holy Trinity v. The United States*; 143 U.S. 457, 471 (1892); cited by D. James Kennedy and Jerry Newcombe, *What if the Bible Had Never Been Written* (Nashville: Thomas Nelson, 1998), 98.

EPILOGUE

[47] Hart, 64.

[48] B. F. Morris, *Christian Life and Character of the Civil Institutions of the United States* (Philadelphia: George W. Childs, 1861), 147.

[49] Joseph Story, *A Familiar Exposition of the Constitution of the United States* (New York: Harper & Brothers, 1847), 259-261; cited by David Barton, *A Spiritual Heritage Tour of the United States Capital* (Aledo, TX: WallBuilders, 2000), 90.

[50] Mark A. Noll, *A History of Christianity in the United States and Canada* (Grand Rapids: Eerdmans, 1992), 394.

[51] Hart, 306.

[52] http://www.heritage.org/research/lecture/2011/06/did-america-have-a-christian-founding